My Heart In Your Hands

Toni Stefano

My Heart In Your Hands © 2023 Toni
Stefano

All rights reserved.

No part of this publication may be
reproduced, stored in a retrieval system, or
transmitted, in any form or by any means,
electronic, mechanical, photocopying,
recording or otherwise, without the prior
written permission of the presenters.

Toni Stefano asserts the moral right to be
identified as author of this work.

Presentation by *BookLeaf Publishing*

Web: www.bookleafpub.com

E-mail: info@bookleafpub.com

ISBN: 9789357740166

First edition 2023

*I have to dedicate this book to my Dad
Ronnie Stefano, as losing him truly ignited
my writing passion. He will always have a
very special place in my heart.*

ACKNOWLEDGEMENT

Thank you to my Husband Dave, my Mum Adele and to my 2 children Talia & Ronnie. You all give me so much support and encouragement, and I adore all of you.

PREFACE

I first realised I had a flare for poetry when my Dad died in 2005, aged 41. I was just 22 and very much struggled to express how I was feeling. One day I sat at the computer and wrote a poem explaining exactly how I felt, which is the first poem in this book. I found it easier to write poems to voice my pain than to say it out loud. I've started with poems about my Dad as this is really where my poem journey properly started. Every poem I write is from my heart, and is a part of my own journey. I hope you enjoy them.

My Dad, My Hero

When I was down you always helped and told
me everything would be ok,
We laughed, we joked, and you brightened up
my day,
But now when I need you the most you're not
here, you're the reason I'm sad,
Please come and take these feelings away, I feel
so bad,
My heart has been broken and will it ever be
repaired?
I didn't ever imagine feeling like this, I'm in
despair,
You were such a major part of my life, and now
you are gone,
I feel so empty, will this feeling last very long?
A light inside me went out the day you died, and
will never be re-lit,
My life feels like a hole I have fallen into, but
can't get out of it,
Why did you get lost in life, why couldn't you
find your way?
But I know you're not suffering now and
that's a consolation in some way,
I know I made you happy, and you made me
happy too,

I love you very much, and I'm so proud of you,
It may seem like you are gone, but really you are there,
You're the sun when it's been raining, you're the breeze in my hair,
I know I will see you again, but not for a long time,
I will meet you where you are now, and we will be fine,
Until then stay happy, and please look after me,
I will keep you in my heart, and there you will always be.

Why??

3

A life so short, but so well lived,
You had so much to offer, so much to give.
A character you were, and always will be,
'Vito' some called you, but you were Dad to me.
A face around town, someone to fear,
But behind closed doors you shed many tears.
Handsome, emotional, funny and kind,
You were so clever, you had a great mind.
Why did someone so good die so young?
It doesn't seem fair, you were only 41.

Trying To Be Strong

It's easy for me to sit here and cry,
It's easy for me to keep wondering why?
But where will it get me, what good is that?
One thing I know is you're not coming back.
So I have to keep smiling, and try to be strong,
Keep thinking of you so your memory lives on,
Think of the good times, and smile because you
lived,
Think of the love and kindness you did give,
I'll remember the good times that we shared,
And how you made me feel safe if I was scared.
I'll laugh at the memories, the fun that we had,
Most of all I'll be proud that you were my Dad.

Christmas Without You

At Christmas time you're on my mind, as you
are throughout the year,
Wishing I could see your face, wishing you were
here.
As family gets together to enjoy the festive
season,
I feel a sadness in my heart, for that you are the
reason.
It doesn't get any easier, as the years pass by,
I try to keep a smile on my face, I try hard not to
cry,
It's impossible not to miss you, I think of you
with love,
I hope you are looking down on us, from your
cloud up above,
So many memories of you at Christmas, so
many that make me smile,
So many more we could have had, if only you
could have stayed a while.
But my memories of you are always with me,
even though we are apart,
I know that I will carry you forever in my heart.

Light At The End Of The Tunnel

Life has already changed so much, just knowing
you are there,
We can't wait to show you just how loved you
are, how much we care.
We think of you when we go to sleep at the end
of every day,
When we open our eyes, you're always in our
thoughts in some way.
We imagine what you will look like, what sort of
person will you be?
Will you look like Mummy? Or more like your
Daddy?
We are so excited to meet you, more than you
will ever know,
Our darling little baby, we look forward to
watching you grow.

The Lives That Were Not Meant To Be

The constant disappointment, the constant despair,
The constant longing for a child who wasn't there.
Wondering would it ever be our turn?
To be a Mummy and a Daddy, we were ready to learn.
It was easy to get pregnant, every time it happened so fast,
But each time the pregnancy just didn't last.
So much prodding and poking, so many blood tests and scans,
You think you can't deal with these things but when you have to you can.
Some of the things people said, I'm sure they were trying to be kind,
But some of them made me go out of my mind!
"At least you can get pregnant!".. yes I should be grateful for that I know,
But how do you think it feels that my body won't let my baby grow?
"Well it wasn't a real baby at the end of the day",

It was my baby no matter how small, saying that
is not ok!
It was a hope, a dream, of a life that was to be,
Someone for me to cherish, someone who would
be a part of me.
When you lose a baby you remember them
forever,
They are a small part of your memory, a part that
you alway treasure.

Early Days With Talia

It changes your life, being a mum
Carrying another person in your tum
Giving life to this perfect little gift
Even if the labour wasn't that swift!
A little person totally dependent on you
It's a wonderful feeling, and slightly scary too
Getting to know my little girl
Even though I already love her all the world
Finding out what makes her tick
And being there for her when she's sick
I will always put her before myself
It makes me happy, it's better than wealth
Thinking of her makes me feel warm inside
There is nothing bigger than a mother's pride.

Baby Number Two!

I always knew I wanted to be a Mum
But when I thought of babies, I only imagined
one
But as Talia grew, it soon became clear
That we would love another little human of ours
here
We had more love to give, there was room for
one more
Another little person for us to adore
And so Ronnie has arrived, a beautiful baby
boy!
He's completed our world, he's our pride and joy
A girl and a boy, we feel as blessed as can be
After all the heartache, I'm now a very happy
Mummy!

My Passion

I'm raising 2 little people, I have a very
important role,
Being a mum requires my heart and my soul,
It's a job that I love, and feel blessed to enjoy,
My whole world is my little girl and my little
boy,
But there were times when it wasn't easy, when I
doubted myself,
Feeling so low is never good for your health,
Every day was the same, the washing was
endless,
And watching children's tv was making me
senseless,
One day I had a brainwave, poems I could write,
It's something I enjoy and I can do it day or
night,
It's fits around the kids, and I can do it all from
home,
It's something where I'm 'me' again, something
to call my own,
So now although my first job will always be as
Mum,
My writing keeps me sane enough to be a bit
more fun!

1st May, The Dreaded Day

The dreaded day is here again
1st May, I can't wait for it to end
Years pass by, but it still hurts as much
If only you were still here to see, here to touch
I miss your cuddles, I miss your laugh
I miss seeing you walk up the path
So much has happened, so much has changed
I wonder what you would have made of the
world today
There's many things that would have made you
proud
I hope you can see everything from up on your
cloud
Your grandchildren know about you, and always
will
It's not the same as them knowing you in person,
but still
I try to explain what a character you were
A lot of you has passed down to him and to her
Talia has your sarcasm, and definitely your wit
Ronnie has your charm and cheekiness, I sure
remember it
It's been many years now, but it feels like
yesterday
I will never forget the day you went away

But I try not to focus just on that time
You had a great life, and as a Dad you were
mine
For that I am grateful, and that will always be
true
Until we meet again Dad, I love you.

Childhood

My daughter asked me about my childhood,
'Tell me about it' she said,
I struggled to find the right words, even though
the memories are in my head.
I found it hard to express to her, how life had
been back then,
So simple but so happy… she asked me again
and again.

Summers in the garden, bonfire night parties out
there too,
There wasn't many walks to the park, I can
remember only one trip to the zoo.
No trampoline centres, not even a soft play,
We all made our own fun in our own way.

There wasn't any woods nearby, horse riding no
I never did,
We didn't go to that many places when I was a
kid.
I didn't have a sandpit in my back garden, I
didn't have a pool,
But my childhood honestly was really kinda
cool.

I played with my toys in my bedroom, an only
child I played alone,
I was very happy doing that, and I was content
to be at home.
When something was on the tv, you watched it
or missed out,
But it didn't really matter, that wasn't what life
was about.

Playing in the street with your mates,
Our parents let us have more freedom which was
great.
There wasn't as many worries as there are today,
Parents had a little peace and we just loved to
play.

We would be out there for hours, no cares in the
world,
Playing with all the other boys and girls.
When dinner was ready, Mum would stand at the
door and shout,
You went straight in for your dinner, you didn't
mess about.

So when I tried to explain to my daughter all
about when I was young,
It seems so very simple, but I had so much fun.
I didn't have the internet, an iPad or a phone,
I was an only child but I never felt alone.

My kids were playing out on the street recently-
a water fight with a friend,
They were having so much fun til the sun went
down, didn't want the day to end.
I said to my Daughter.. "Remember you asked
me about my childhood?,
"It was THIS" … and I think she understood.

To My Mum

Of all the poems that I write there is only one
That means as much to me as writing one for my
Mum
A beautiful woman, both inside and out
Cares so much for us, of that there's no doubt
Puts everyone else first, she's always been that
way
Makes us laugh with some of the scatty things
she does say!
She's cuddly, funny, lovable and sweet
One of the kindest women you will have the
pleasure to meet
She's always been creative and has a flair for art
Should have more confidence in herself, she
doesn't realise she's smart!
Her Grandchildren are very obviously her world
She adores Ronnie her handsome boy and Talia
her pretty girl
It's lovely to see how much she enjoys being a
Nan
She can do anything she puts her mind to, if she
can't do it no one can!
I couldn't wish for a better Mum if I tried
She's always been my rock, and she makes me
feel so much pride.

Talia's Star

A little girl called Talia was off to her bed
It's time to sleep now, her mummy had said
A kiss and a cuddle, and then its goodnight
A quick bedtime story, then off goes the light
Now all is dark and quiet, but Talia is not asleep
And from out of her bed she is starting to creep
She goes to the window, looks up to the sky
There's a bright shining star up ever so high!
I want that star in my hand, Talia decides
Then the star starts to fly, down from the sky!
It comes to the window and taps on the glass
"Can I come in?" the little star asks
Talia opens the window and in comes the star
"Phew!" it says, panting, "I've come down so
far!"
It jumps in Talia's hand and she squeals in
delight
"Shhh" says the star, "We'll give your mum a
fright!"
So the two of them talk quietly, and even sing
songs
But then Talia realises that something is wrong!
The star's light is fading, it's beginning to dim!
"Help!" cries the star, "I don't know what's
happening!"

"I have always shone bright, when I was up
high"
"I'm one of the brightest stars to have lived in
the sky!"
Talia was worried, but what could be done?
The star needed help, this wasn't much fun!
But then an idea popped into her head
Maybe the star needed to be back in the sky
instead!
"I don't think you're supposed to be here", she
said to the star
"You need to be back in the sky, up ever so far"
"I think that will help you, to get back your
light"
"But how are we going to get you back up into
the night?"
"Hmm" said the star, "I'm really not sure"
"It's not like I can just easily walk out the door!"
Talia closed her eyes, and held the star tight
Everything was quiet, and she wished with all
her might
Please send the star back, to his home in the sky
It's not fair for his light to fade and die!
Talia opened her eyes, and the star wasn't there!
She was still in her bedroom, but her hands were
bare
Then she went to the window, looked up to sky
There's a bright shining star, up ever so high!

It's the brightest in the sky, so her wish had
come true!
The star startled to twinkle, as if saying "thank
you!"
Talia was happy, but she gave a big yawn
She was feeling tired now, and soon it would be
dawn!
She had better get some sleep, so she crawled
back into bed
Got under the cover, and lay down her sleepy
head.

Ronnie The Drummer

Ronnie was getting tired, it had been a long day
He had worked hard at school, and enjoyed his play
Now it was almost bedtime, for a while it had been dark
"I'm not ready for bed yet Mummy!" said Ronnie, "can we go to the park?"
"It's too late now" explained his Mum, as she stroked his head
"It's time for you to go to bed!"
Ronnie wasn't happy, he still wanted to play!
He wondered if his Mum would let him stay up a while, what else could he say?
"Mummy, I really need to practice on my drums!"
Ronnie loved his drum set, he found music so much fun!
"Ok", sighed his Mum, "but only for a while"
She really couldn't help but smile.
So they went up to Ronnie's room, and he sat on his stool
Picked up his drum sticks, feeling super cool
Started to play, he was a rocker in a band!
The music was flowing through the sticks from his hands!

He nodded his head along with the music,
closing his eyes
Ronnie always felt the music, this was no
surprise
He could imagine himself on a stage, playing to
a crowd
Bashing and crashing, at a concert that was loud!
The audience were cheering, clapping with glee
Dancing along to the music happily
He was a Rock Star, yes it was true!
Then.. "Ronnie it's now definitely bed time for
you!"
"Ah Mum!" moaned Ronnie, "you ruined my
show!"
Mum laughed as she said "Come on, into bed
you go!"
Ronnie knew now was the end of the day
But he was happy that he got a chance to jam, a
chance to play!
Laying in his bed he whispered low
"Night night drums! See you tomorrow!"

For Dave, Love Talia & Ronnie

We love how crazy you are and how you make
us giggle,
We love it when you chase us and then we get
tiggles!
Riding on your shoulders, climbing on your
back,
We know you feel like you are always getting us
drinks and a snack.
We may sometimes push our boundaries, and
sometimes drive you mad,
But we absolutely adore you and are so glad you
are our Dad.
You are such good fun to be with, we love
spending time with you,
We appreciate how hard you work and
everything that you do.
Watching films together, and singing silly songs,
You make us feel very safe, you are so big and
strong.
It's plain to see how much you love us, we know
we are your world,
You are our world too, we are so glad we are
your little boy and girl.

We hope you know how special you are, and
also very smart,
You are definitely our hero, and we love you
with all of our hearts.

Uncle Barry's Poem

When I think back to my early years, you were always there
You babysat me often, I remember your love and care
I remember you at family parties, Barry Norman I called you one time
What a lovely Uncle you were, I'm glad that you were mine
A kind and gentle person, so often misunderstood
If only things were different, I would change it if I could
You taught me to ride a bike, memories to treasure
Your funny and silly humour will stay with me forever
I'm sad that I never knew how things were for you in your final years
I wish I could have helped, now there is only sadness and tears
58 is way too young, it shouldn't have been your time just yet
Thank you for being you Barry, for being someone I'll never forget

A Poem for Nanny Sheila

A wonderful Nanny who loved us more than we
know
We were her pride and joy, we wish she didn't
have to go
She loved to bake cakes with us and do lots of
crafts too
Going round her house there was always
something to do
Taking us on days out, she couldn't do enough
She was someone we could turn to when times
were tough
Our Nanny Sheila loved to give us cuddles, we
wish we could have one more
We were her pride and joy, it was us she did
adore
We were very lucky to have her, if only for a
while
The fact she was our Nanny really makes us
smile
We will never forget her, even though we are
apart
Throughout our whole life she will be safely in
our hearts

Remembering You

Remembering you is never easy, it hurts my
heart sometimes,
But it's something I can never stop doing, for to
forget you would be a lie,
You will always be in my head, and always in
my heart,
I've had to move on with my life, but it was hard
to know where to start,
Time is not a healer, my broken heart will never
mend,
It's a pain I have to live with, sometimes it feels
like it will never end,
But life does go on without those who have to
leave our side,
And all we can do is hope that they are watching
us with pride,
I'm happy that you were here, and that I could
call you mine,
Happy for the memories, to me they will always
shine,
And even though I miss you, more and more
each day,
I'll keep you safe in my heart, and there you will
always stay.

www.ingramcontent.com/pod-product-compliance
Lightning Source LLC
LaVergne TN
LVHW021332200726
843509LV00014B/2501